Songs of *Inspiration, Perseverance & Hope*

25 Contemporary, Uplifting Songs

Alfred Cares.
$1 from the sale of this book
will be donated to cancer research.

W9-CFN-385

Alfred Music
P.O. Box 10003
Van Nuys, CA 91410-0003
alfred.com

Printed in USA.

*No part of this book shall be reproduced, arranged, adapted, recorded, publicly performed, stored in a retrieval system,
or transmitted by any means without written permission from the publisher. In order to comply with copyright laws, please apply for
such written permission and/or license by contacting the publisher at alfred.com/permissions.*

ISBN-10: 0-7390-9994-9
ISBN-13: 978-0-7390-9994-0

Cover Photos
Pink breast cancer awareness ribbon: © Shutterstock / Atesevich
Floral background frames with flowering branch: © Shutterstock / Filipchuk Oleg

Foreword

Cancer is and has been a devastating disease with no boundaries. Hardly a family has not been touched with the loss of a loved one. While much progress has been made in dealing with the problem, a true cure for all cancers remains elusive. However, early detection and a steady stream of new drugs and treatments have given hope to many and allowed a large number to live full and productive lives. This book of *Songs of Inspiration, Perseverance & Hope* is dedicated to those who are fighting the battle, and also to those families who were less fortunate.

Among the individuals who have fought valiantly and lost their battle are two very special women who were closely associated with Alfred Music. Gwen Bailey-Harbour, age 49, was an Alfred Senior Vice President who died of breast cancer; Jean Gordon Vicks, age 49, was the wife of the President of a major printing supplier, Vicks Litho, and died of thyroid cancer. Gwen is survived by her husband and two children; Jean is survived by her husband and three children.

While these are the facts, they tell nothing of their courage, spirit, and ability to continue on with their lives as mothers and wives while fighting against this unforgiving disease. Their passing was devastating to all who knew them.

What we have done in this book is to include many of the songs that *inspired* Gwen and Jean to *persevere* in their struggle, and to keep *hoping* a cure would eventually arrive to save those who shared their illness. It has not yet – but with your help, someday it will save others. This special collection of contemporary, uplifting songs gives the pianist an opportunity to play and sing for those in need.

Since 1985, October has become *Breast Cancer Awareness Month*. It is an annual international health campaign organized by major breast cancer charities to increase the awareness of the disease and to raise funds for research into its cause.

Though thyroid cancer is not as well known, the rate of diagnosis is increasing faster than that of any other cancer. By 2020, it is expected to be the fourth most common cancer. In 2013, 45,000 women will be diagnosed with thyroid cancer.

To help raise funds for research, Alfred will contribute $1 from the sale of each book—50% to Memorial Sloan-Kettering and 50% to the International Thyroid Oncology Group. There is a cure coming, hopefully sooner than later. Until then, it will take all of our combined efforts to make certain a cure for all is reached.

Contents

Anyway

Words and Music by
MARTINA McBRIDE, BRAD WARREN
and BRETT WARREN

Moderately slow ballad ♩ = 66

al-ways turn out like__ I think it should,__ but I do it an-y-way.__

__ I do it an-y-way.__

Verse 2:

2. This world's__gone cra - zy, and it's hard to be - lieve__ that to -

mor - row will__ be bet - ter than__ to - day._____ Be - lieve it

Badlands

Words and Music by
BRUCE SPRINGSTEEN

Verse 1 (sing 1st time only):

lights out to-night, trou-ble in the heart-land, got a head-on col-li-sion smash-

Verse 2 (sing 2nd time only):

in' in the fields 'til___ you get your back burned. Work-in' 'neath the wheel, hell,

Whoa,_ whoa,_ whoa,_ whoa._ *(Guitar solo…*

(Tenor Sax. solo…

...end solo)

Mm,_____ mm,_____

mm,_____ mm._____

_____ For the ones who had a no-tion on a no-tion deep in-side, that it

cresc. *mp*

I Am Beautiful

Words and Music by
JOLEEN BELLE, CANDICE GLOVER
and JADEN MICHAELS

Moderately slow ♩ = 70

(with pedal)

Mmm, ___ mmm. ___

1. You say I sound sil-ly when I laugh real ___ loud.
2. You say I'll nev-er be good e - nough. ___

Talk a-bout my day ___ and you tune me out. ___
Knock me down, ___ won't help me up. ___

I Am Beautiful - 5 - 1

Chorus:

Bridge Over Troubled Water

Words and Music by
PAUL SIMON

Moderately slow ♩ = 84

(with pedal)

Verse 1:

1. When you're wear - y, feel - in'___

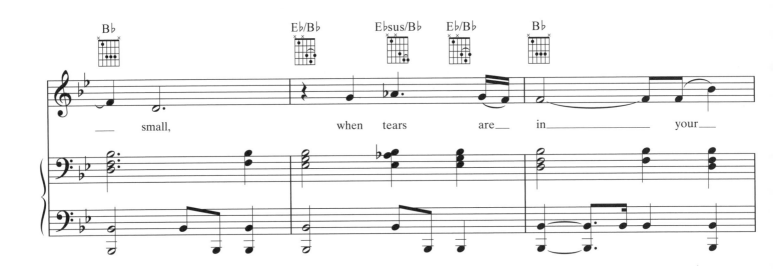

___ small, when tears are___ in_____ your___

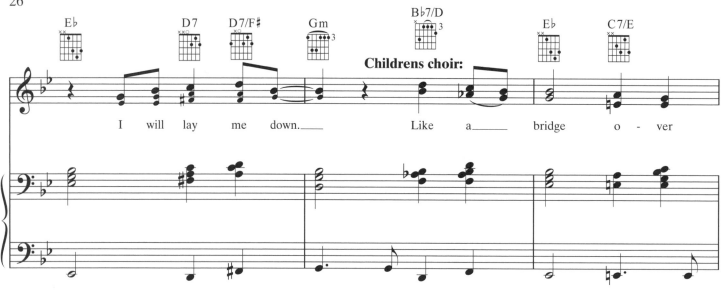

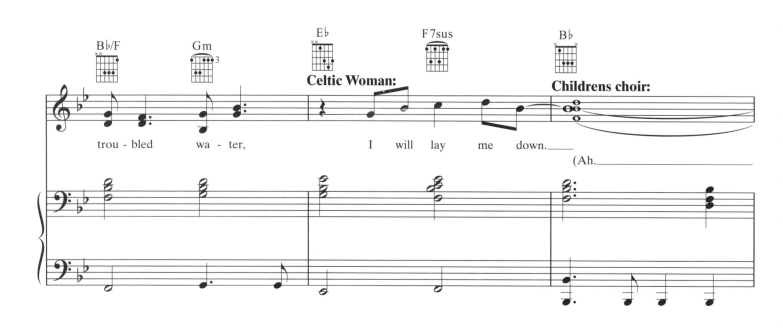

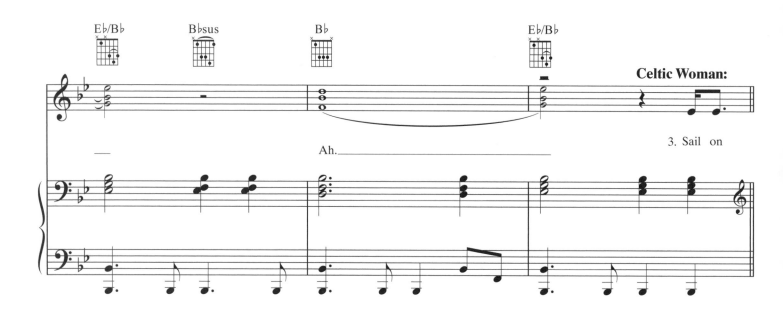

A Change Is Gonna Come

Words and Music by
SAM COOKE

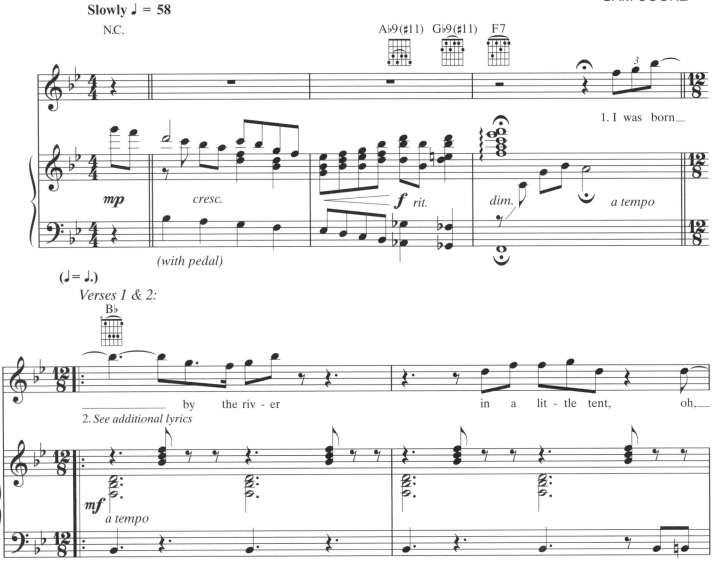

Verse 2:
It's been too hard living but I'm afraid to die
'Cause I don't know what's up there beyond the sky.
It's been a long, a long time comin',
But I know, oh-oo-oh,
A change gonna come, oh yes, it will.

Verse 4:
There've been times that I thought
I couldn't last for long
But now I think I'm able to carry on
It's been a long, a long time comin',
but I know, oh-oo-oh, a change gonna come, oh yes, it will.

Count on Me

Words and Music by
PETER HERNANDEZ, PHILIP LAWRENCE
and ARI LEVINE

Moderately ♩ = 88

Uh - huh.____ 1. If you

Verse:

ev - er find your - self stuck in the mid-dle of the sea,____ I'll sail_
toss - in' and you're turn-in', and you just__ can't__ fall a - sleep,____ I'll sing.

____ the world_ to find____ you._____ If you
____ a song__ be - side____ you._____ And if you

*Harmony 2nd time

*Sing cue notes last time.

Don't Stop Believin'

Words and Music by
JONATHAN CAIN, NEAL SCHON
and STEVE PERRY

Feels Like Home

Words and Music by
RANDY NEWMAN

Verse 2:
A window breaks down a long, dark street,
And a siren wails in the night.
But I'm alright 'cause I have you here with me,
And I can almost see, through the dark there's a light.
If you'd knew how much this moment means to me,
And how long I've waited for your touch.
If you knew how happy you are making me,
I've never thought I'd love anyone so much.
(To Chorus:)

Greatest Love Of All

Words by LINDA CREED
Music by MICHAEL MASSER

Chorus:

Imagine

Words and Music by
JOHN LENNON

you may say_____ I'm a dream-er, but I'm not the on - ly one.___

I hope some day_____ you'll join us_____

and the world____ will be as one.   and the world____ will live as one.___

rit.

I'm One

Words and Music by
PETER TOWNSHEND

Moderately ♩ = 96

(with pedal)

Verse 1:

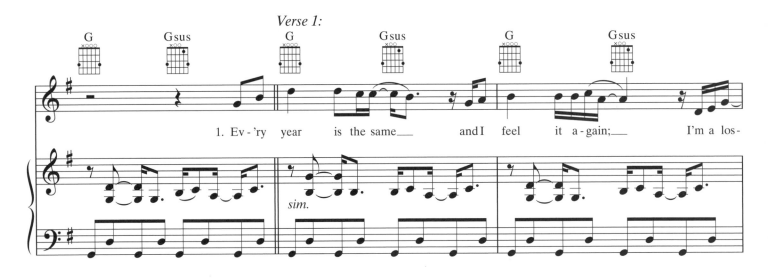

1. Ev-'ry year is the same___ and I feel it a-gain;___ I'm a los-

sim.

er, no chance to win.___ Leaves___start fall-ing,

I'm One - 5 - 1

56

Verse 2:

2. Where do you get those blue, blue jeans;

fad-ed, patched, se-cret, so tight? Where do you get that

walk, oh so lean; your shoes and yer shirts all just right. I'm

In My Daughter's Eyes

Words and Music by
JAMES SLATER

Slowly ♩ = 72

Verses 1 & 2:

1. In my daugh-ter's

eyes,   I am___ a he-ro,___   I am
eyes,   ev-'ry-one___ is e-qual,___   dark-ness

In My Daughter's Eyes - 5 - 1

Bridge:

Land of Hope and Dreams

Words and Music by
BRUCE SPRINGSTEEN

Moderate rock ♩ = 112

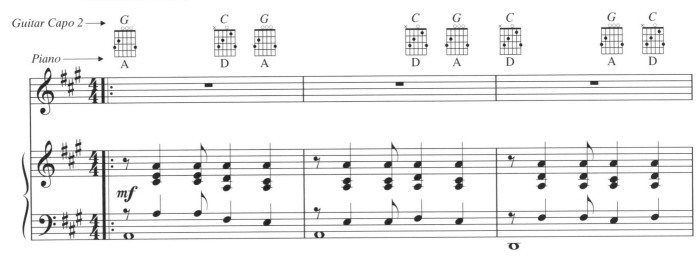

* Cue size notes played 2nd time only

Land of Hope and Dreams - 11 - 2

of hope and dreams.
of hope and dreams.

This train... car-ries saints and sin-ners. This

train... bells of free - dom ring - in'.

Sax solo:

Let There Be Peace on Earth

Words and Music by
SY MILLER and JILL JACKSON

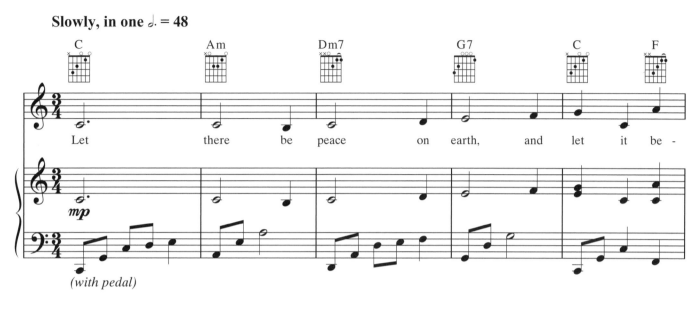

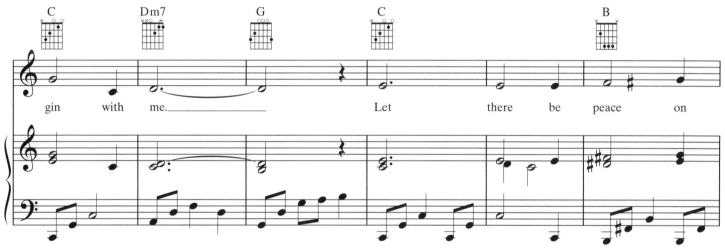

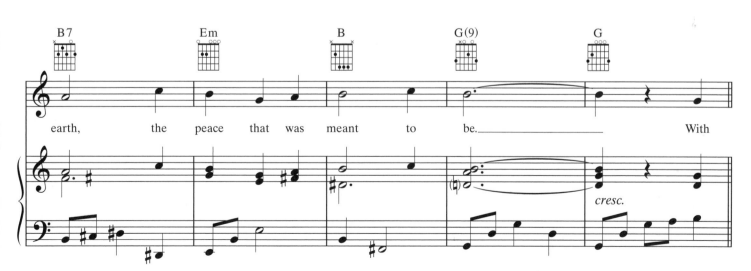

Let There Be Peace on Earth - 3 - 1

Laugh and Be Happy

Words and Music by
RANDY NEWMAN

Fast, jazzy - vaudevillian feel

(semi-spoken:) I know what's go-ing on here, ain't no great mys-ter-y. Y' - all have lost faith in your-selves, It's (more sung:)

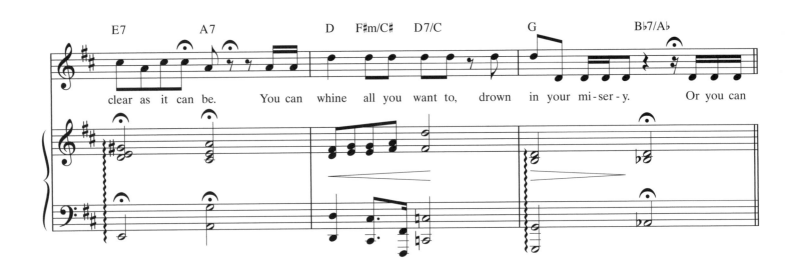

clear as it can be. You can whine all you want to, drown in your mi-ser-y. Or you can

Fast rag ♩ = 132

lis-ten to me, lis-ten to me. Laugh and be hap-py, don't you

sempre ad lib. fast eccentric rag style...

82

My Love Will Not Let You Down

Words and Music by
BRUCE SPRINGSTEEN

Verse 2:
At night I walk the streets looking for romance,
But I always end up stumbling in a half-trance.
I search for connection in some new eyes,
But they're hard for protection from too many dreams passed by.
I see you standing across the room watching me without a sound.
Well, I'm gonna push my way through that crowd,
I'm gonna tear all your walls down.
Tear all your walls down.
(To Chorus:)

Verse 3:
(Measures 1-16 Inst. solo ad lib.)
Well, hold still now, darling, hold still for God's sake.
'Cause I got me a promise I ain't afraid to make.
(To Chorus:)

Only Hope

Words and Music by
JONATHAN FOREMAN

*Original recording in C# minor.

Only Hope - 7 - 1

Need You Now (How Many Times)

Words and Music by
CHRISTA WELLS, LUKE SHEETS
and TIFFANY ARBUCKLE

Slow pop groove ♩ = 66

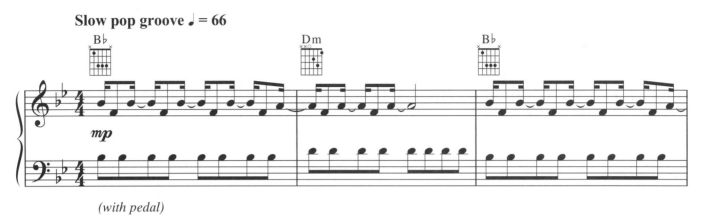

(with pedal)

Verse 1:

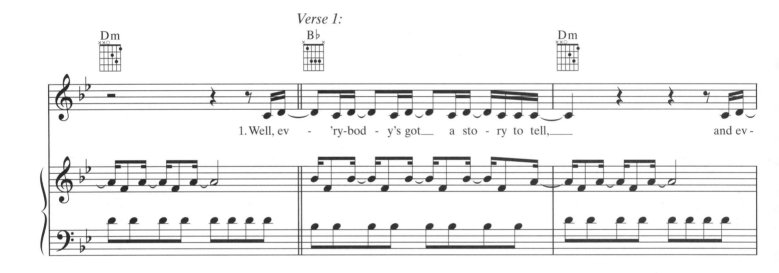

1. Well, ev - 'ry-bod - y's got__ a sto - ry to tell,__ and ev-

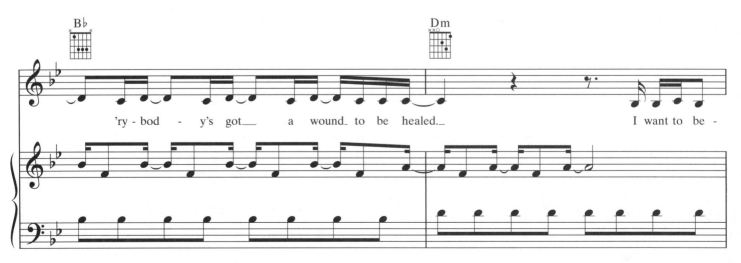

'ry - bod - y's got__ a wound__ to be healed.__ I want to be-

Need You Now - 6 - 1

Bridge:

The Prayer

Italian Lyric by
ALBERTO TESTA and TONY RENIS

Words and Music by
CAROLE BAYER SAGER and DAVID FOSTER

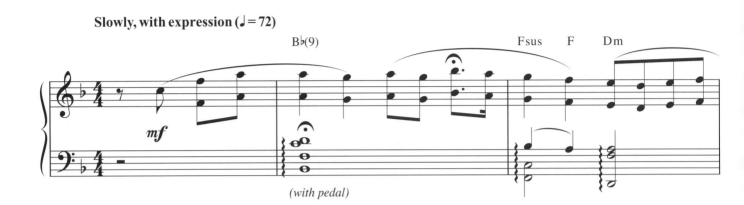

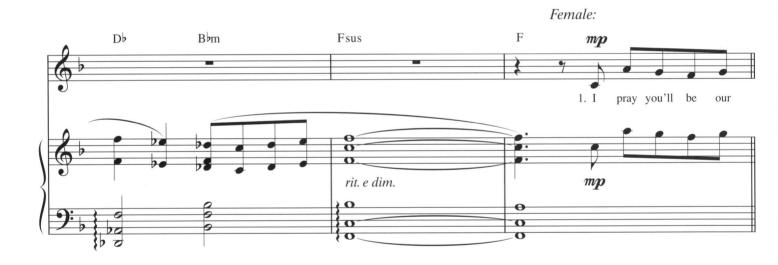

The Prayer - 8 - 5

So Small

Words and Music by
CARRIE UNDERWOOD, HILLARY LINDSEY
and LUKE LAIRD

Slowly ♩ = 76

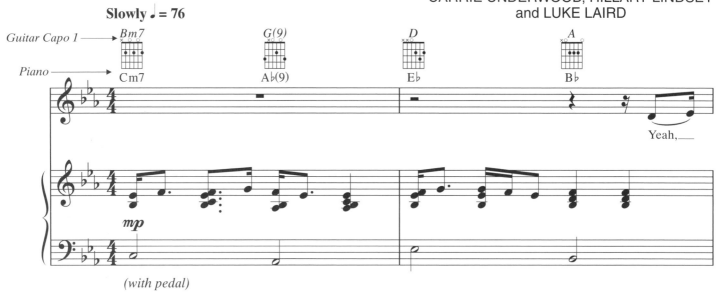

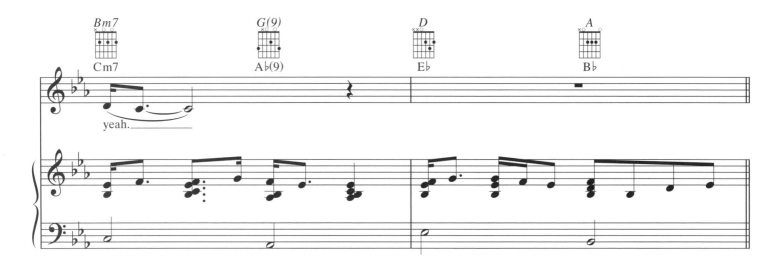

Verse 1:

1. What you got if you ain't_ got love, the kind that_ you just_ want to give a - way?

So Small - 8 - 1

Thank You

Words and Music by
JIMMY PAGE and ROBERT PLANT

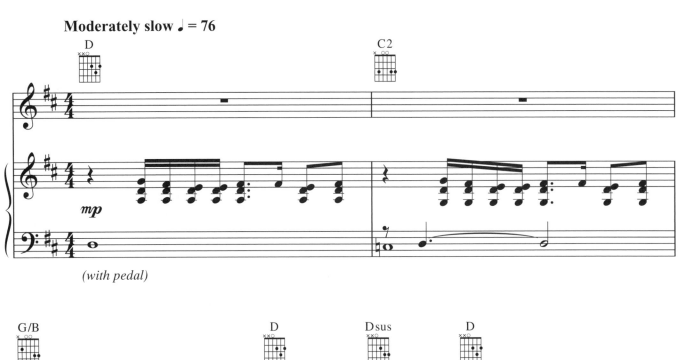

(with pedal)

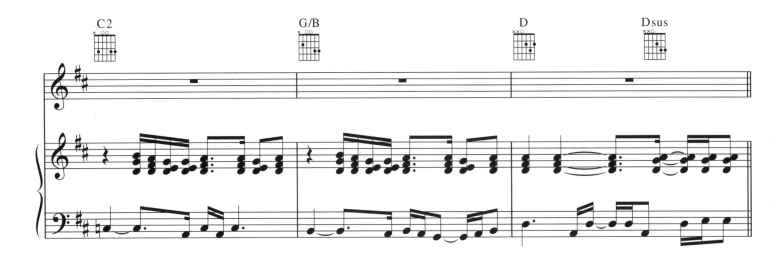

Thank You - 7 - 1

to_____ the sea,___ there will___ still be you___ and me.

Organic solo:

Repeat ad lib. and fade

Verse 2:
And so today my world, it smiles,
Your hand in mine, we walk the miles.
Thanks to you, it will be done,
For you to me are the only one.
Happiness, no more be sad, happiness, I'm glad.

Waitin' on a Sunny Day

Words and Music by
BRUCE SPRINGSTEEN

Am

there ain't a cloud in the sky.___ Must___ have been a tear from your eye,___
in' with the rain fall - in' down.___ I'm half a par - ty in a one dog___ town,
by, well they come to us all.___ Sure as the tick - in' of the clock on the wall,___

F   C

___ ev - 'ry-thing will be o - kay._____
___ I need you to chase these blues a - way._____
___ sure as the turn-in' of the night in-to day._____

G   C

It's fun - ny,   thought___ I felt a sweet sum-mer breeze.___
With - out___ you   I'm a drum - mer girl that can't keep a beat,___
Your smile,___ girl,   brings___ the morn-in' light to my eyes,___

Am   F

___ Must___ have been you sigh-in' so deep.___   Don't wor-
___ an ice cream truck on a de-sert-ed___ street.___   I hope.
___ lifts___ a - way the blues when I rise.___   I hope.

Coda

What a Wonderful World

Words and Music by
GEORGE DAVID WEISS and BOB THIELE

You Light Up My Life

Words and Music by
JOE BROOKS

You Raise Me Up

Words and Music by
ROLF LOVLAND and
BRENDAN GRAHAM

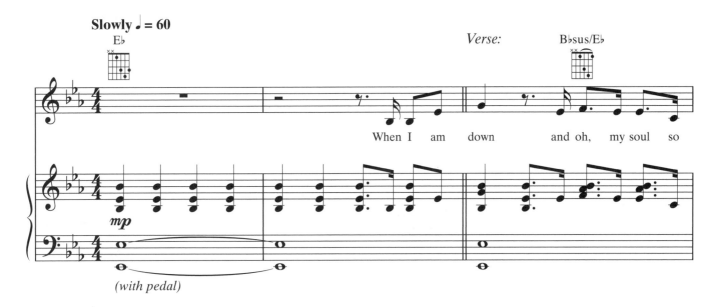

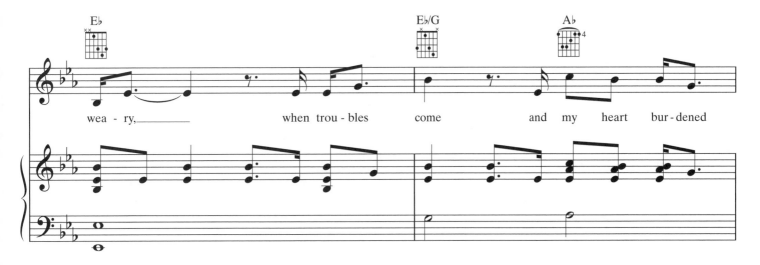

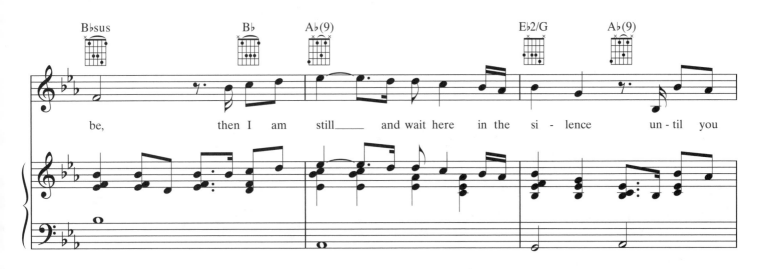

You Raise Me Up - 5 - 1